100 FACTS YOU SHOULD KNOW

EXTREME EARTH

By Anna Claybourne

 Gareth Stevens
PUBLISHING

Please visit our website, **www.garethstevens.com**. For a free color catalog of all our high-quality books, call toll free 1-800-542-2595 or fax 1-877-542-2596.

Claybourne, Anna.
Extreme earth / by Anna Claybourne.
p. cm. — (100 facts)
Includes index.
ISBN 978-1-4824-1304-5 (pbk.)
ISBN 978-1-4824-1262-8 (6-pack)
ISBN 978-1-4824-1464-6 (library binding)
1. Climatic extremes — Juvenile literature. 2. Weather — Juvenile literature. I. Claybourne, Anna. II. Title.
QC981.3 C53 2015
551.55—d23

Published in 2015 by
Gareth Stevens Publishing
111 East 14th Street, Suite 349
New York, NY 10003

Copyright © 2014 Miles Kelly Publishing Ltd

Publishing Director: Belinda Gallagher
Creative Director: Jo Cowan
Editorial Assistant: Sarah Parkin
Volume Designer: Simon Lee

ACKNOWLEDGEMENTS
The publishers would like to thank the following artists who have contributed to this book:
Richard Burgess, Mike Foster
All other artworks from the Miles Kelly Artwork Bank

The publishers would like to thank the following sources for the use of their photographs:
Cover photograph: Roza/Fotolia; Page 6 Gary Braasch/Corbis; 8(l) Topham Picturepoint/TopFoto.co.uk, (r) QiangBa DanZhen/Fotolia.com; 11 Yann Arthus-Bertrand/Corbis; 12 David Samuel Robbins/Corbis; 14 Steve Vidler/Photolibrary; 15(l) Albo/Fotolia.com, (r) Pablo Corral V/Corbis; 16(t) JTB Photo/Photolibrary, (b) NASA; 18(t) Robert Dowling/Corbis, (b) Stephen Alvarez/Getty Images; 19 Javier Trueba/MSF/Science Photo Library; 20 Phil Degginger/Photolibrary; 21(t) JTB Photo/Photolibrary, (b) Paul Chesley/Getty Images; 22 Jeremy Horner/Corbis; 23(l) NASA, (r) NASA; 25(b) Frans Lemmens/Zefa/Corbis; 26(t) Tim Davis/Corbis, (b) Rick Price/Corbis; 29(t) Paul A. Souders/Corbis, (b) Colin Monteath/Photolibrary; 32 Image Source/Corbis; 35(l) Nick Hawkes/Ecoscene, (r) Peter Menzel/Science Photo Library; 36(t) Jim Reed/FLPA, (b) Denis Balibouse/Reuters; 37 AFP/Getty Images; 38(t) flucas@Fotolia.com, (m) Aurora/Getty Images; 39 Reuters/Corbis; 40 Eric Nguyen/Corbis; 42 Warren Faidley/Corbis; 44(t) NASA, (b) Mike Goldwater/Getty Images; 45(t) Sipa Press/Rexfeatures; 46 C A.Ishokon-UNEP/Still Pictures; 47(b) NOAA/Science Photo Library
All other photographs are from: Corel, digitalSTOCK, digitalvision, iStockphoto.com, John Foxx, PhotoAlto, PhotoDisc, PhotoEssentials, PhotoPro, Stockbyte

Printed in the United States of America

CPSIA compliance information: Batch CS15GS: For further information contact Gareth Stevens, New York, New York at 1-800-542-2595.

Contents

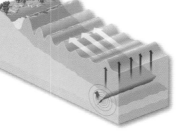

Our extreme Earth

1 **The Earth is a planet of extremes.** At the North and South Poles, freezing temperatures reach as low as –40°F (–40°C). Meanwhile, hot water gushes out from the seabed at over 750°F (400°C). Explorers trek to the tops of mountains many miles high, and into deep caves thousands of feet underground. Rainforests are drenched by torrential rain every day, while deserts remain dry for years on end. The Earth also regularly explodes, rumbles, roars, and shakes with wild weather, giant waves, earthquakes, and volcanoes.

▼ A wave crashes ashore on rocks at Cape Arago, Oregon, throwing up a huge fountain of spray. Heavy waves can sink boats, smash buildings, and sweep people off the shore.

Climbing high

2 The Earth is covered with a thick layer of rock, or "crust." In some places, sections of crust have squeezed together, forcing their way upwards to make mountains. Mountains often form in a long line or group, called a mountain range. High up, it is cold and windy. This means that the tops of mountains are very icy, snowy, and stormy.

Mount Everest
29,035 feet
(8,850 m)
(Asia)

Mount Kilimanjaro
19,341 feet
(5,895 m)
(Africa)

Mount Cook 12,316 feet (3,754 m) (Oceania)

3 **Mount Everest is the world's highest mountain.** It's on the border between Nepal and China, in the Himalayas mountain range. It is about 29,035 feet (8,850 m) high. The first people to climb to the top of Everest were Edmund Hillary and Tenzing Norgay on May 29, 1953.

4 **The highest mountain on Earth isn't the hardest to climb.** Another peak, K2, is much tougher for mountaineers. At 28,251 feet (8,611 m), it's the world's second-highest mountain. Its steep slopes and swirling storms make it incredibly dangerous. Fewer than 300 people have ever climbed it, and over 65 have died in the attempt.

▲ Edmund Hillary (left) and Tenzing Norgay, photographed in 1953, the year they became the first to climb Mount Everest. Hillary died in 2008.

▶ Mount Everest is so high that climbers have to climb it over several days, stopping at camps along the way.

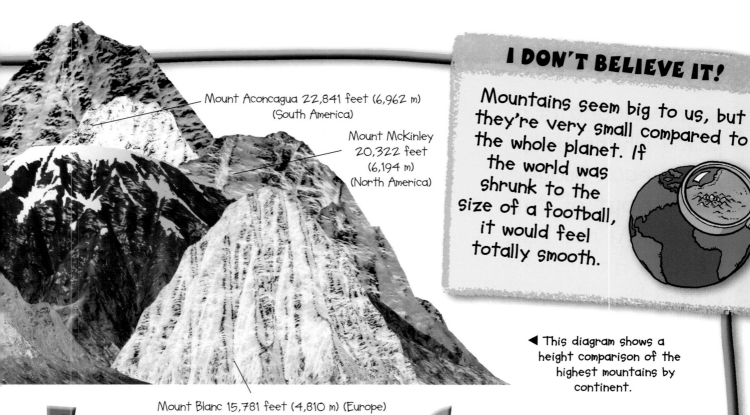

Mount Aconcagua 22,841 feet (6,962 m) (South America)

Mount McKinley 20,322 feet (6,194 m) (North America)

Mount Blanc 15,781 feet (4,810 m) (Europe)

◀ This diagram shows a height comparison of the highest mountains by continent.

5 **Most mountains are shaped like big humps — but a cliff is a sheer drop.** The east face of Great Trango, a mountain in Pakistan, is 4,396 feet (1,340 m) high, making it the tallest vertical cliff in the world. There's another giant cliff on Mount Thor in Canada, with a drop of 4,101 feet (1,250 m). If a pebble fell off one of these cliffs, it would take more than 15 seconds to reach the bottom!

6 **Some people don't just climb to the tops of high mountains — they live there!** The town of Wenzhuan in Tibet, China, is the highest in the world. It is in the Himalayas, 16,732 feet (5,100 m) up – that's over 3 miles (5 km) above sea level! The highest capital city is La Paz in the Andes in Bolivia, South America. It has an altitude (height) of around 11,800 feet (3,600 m).

▶ There are three types of mountains: volcanic, fold, and block.

2. Fold mountains occur when sections of the Earth's crust push against each other, making the land buckle and fold upward.

3. Block mountains occur when sections of the crust split and crack, forming faults where some sections are pushed up higher than others.

1. Volcanic mountains form when hot, liquid rock (lava) erupts through the Earth's crust. As the lava cools, it forms a rocky layer. With each new eruption, another layer is added.

Violent volcanoes

7 A volcano is a place where hot, liquid rock (magma) bursts out of the Earth. At the Earth's surface, magma is called lava. Red-hot lava can be seen flowing or shooting out of a volcano. After a volcano erupts, the lava cools into solid rock. These rocky layers build the volcano higher and higher with each eruption.

▶ In 1980, a massive cloud of lava dust, ash, and hot gas burst out of Mount St. Helens in Washington State.

8 The biggest eruptions happen when pressure builds up underground. The magma pushes up and up, but the crust on top stops it from escaping. The ground bulges and swells, until at last the magma bursts out in a huge explosion. This happened at Mount St. Helens in Washington State in 1980. The explosion was so huge, it blew away half the mountain!

Ash cloud

Flowing lava

Magma chamber

▲ An erupting volcano can release clouds of ash and gas as well as liquid lava.

9 The biggest volcanic eruption ever recorded was the eruption of Mount Tambora in Indonesia in 1815. The eruption was heard on the island of Sumatra, over 1,250 miles (2,012 km) away. Ash from the eruption filled the sky and blocked out sunlight all around the Earth. It made the weather very cold, and people called 1816 "the year without a summer."

▲ The island of Surtsey today, more than 40 years after it appeared out of the sea.

11 A volcano can build a brand-new island! In 1963, smoke and steam began to billow out of the sea near Iceland. A volcano was erupting on the seabed. As the lava and ash piled up, it built a new island. The island was named Surtsey. Gradually, moss, grass, and trees began to grow, and birds and insects began to live there.

10 Volcanoes can be killers. Victims can be burned by hot lava, hit by flying rocks, suffocated under hot ash, or poisoned by gas. After the eruption, ash can mix with rainwater to make fast-flowing mud that can drown whole towns. People are in danger from eruptions because there are many towns and farms close to volcanoes. This is partly because volcanic ash helps to make the land fertile for growing crops.

VINEGAR VOLCANO MODEL

You will need:
vinegar   baking soda   red food coloring
sand   tray   jug   plastic bottle

Put a tablespoon of baking soda in the plastic bottle. Stand the bottle on a tray and make a cone of sand around it. Put a few drops of red food coloring in half a cup of vinegar.

Tip the vinegar into a jug, then pour it into the bottle. In a few moments, the volcano should erupt with red, frothy "lava."

Hot springs and fountains

12 **There are natural hot baths and showers all over the world.** You might think water outdoors is cold, but in some places, water meets hot rock under the ground and gets heated up. It sometimes even boils. The hot water can then make a lake or spring — or even shoot out of the ground like a fountain, forming a geyser.

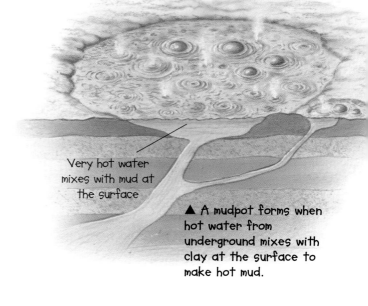

Very hot water mixes with mud at the surface

▲ A mudpot forms when hot water from underground mixes with clay at the surface to make hot mud.

▼ A mudpot, like this one in Myvatn Geothermal Area in Iceland, is a pool of hot, bubbling mud. Some mudpots are boiling hot. Others bubble as hot gases burst up through them.

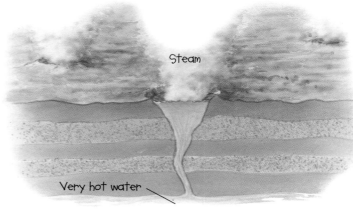

Steam

Very hot water

▲ Sometimes, hot underground water forms steam, which escapes through a hole or crack in the ground. These are called steam vents, or fumaroles.

13 **You shouldn't stand too close to a geyser — even if nothing's happening!** A geyser is a hole in the ground that suddenly shoots out hot water and steam. Under the hole, there is a water-filled chamber. Hot rock beneath it heats the water until it rises back to the surface and erupts in a giant jet of water and steam.

14 Old Faithful is one of the world's most famous geysers. Found in Yellowstone National Park, it gets its name because it erupts on average once every 94 minutes. Its jet of steam and water can reach 180 feet (55 m) high – as high as a 15-story building.

15 Soap helps geysers to erupt. People discovered this when they tried to use hot water pools and geysers to wash their clothes in. Soap disturbs the cold water in the chamber, helping the hot water to burst through.

▶ Strokkur (Icelandic for "churn") is a geyser in Iceland. It erupts regularly, every 5–10 minutes, and can shoot water up to 80 feet (24 m) in the air.

16 Besides geysers, the Earth's hot water can form amazing thermal (hot) springs and pools. They often occur in places where there are lots of volcanoes, such as New Zealand and Japan. Some thermal pools are famous for their beautiful colors. These are caused by millions of bacteria (tiny living things) that live in the very hot water.

I DON'T BELIEVE IT!

Japanese macaque monkeys use thermal springs as hot baths! They live in the mountains of Japan where winters are very cold. They climb into the natural hot pools to keep themselves warm.

▼ When rainwater seeps into the earth, it can be heated by hot rocks underground before rising back up to the surface as hot springs, pools, and geysers.

Rainfall adds to groundwater

Geyser

Hot spring

Cold water travels down

Water is heated by hot rocks

Heated water starts to move upwards

Heat from Earth's interior

Rivers and waterfalls

17 **The Earth is laced with thousands of rivers.** Rivers are channels of water that flow towards the sea. They allow the rain that falls on the land to drain away. Rivers also provide people and animals with drinking water and a place to wash, swim, and fish. A waterfall is a place where a river flows over a rocky ledge and pours down to a lower level.

18 **The world's longest river is the Nile in Africa.** It starts in the area near Lake Victoria and flows north to Egypt, where it opens into the Mediterranean Sea. The journey covers nearly 4,175 miles (6,719 km), and about 99,941 cubic feet (2,830 cu m) of water flows out of the Nile every second. The Nile provides water, a transportation route, and fishing for millions of people. If it wasn't for the Nile, the civilization of ancient Egypt could not have existed.

19 **Although the Nile is the longest river, the Amazon is the biggest.** The Amazon flows from west to east across South America and empties into the Atlantic Ocean. It carries 58 times as much water as the Nile, and about 4,200,000 cubic feet (119,000 cu m) flow out of it each second. In some places, the Amazon is an amazing 25 miles (40 km) wide.

◄ This aerial photo of the Amazon River shows how it twists and loops as it flows through the Amazon rainforest in South America.

▶ At Angel Falls, the world's highest waterfall, the water spreads out into a misty spray as it plunges down the cliff.

◀ This is part of the Grand Canyon, with the Colorado River visible at the bottom of a deep gorge.

20 Angel Falls in Venezuela is the world's highest waterfall, spilling over a drop 3,212 feet (979 m) high. It flows off the side of a very high, flat-topped mountain. Although it's the world's highest waterfall, it's not the biggest. Many waterfalls are much wider and carry more water – including Niagara Falls in North America and Victoria Falls in Africa.

21 Rivers can cut through solid rock. Over thousands of years, as a river flows, it wears away the rock around it. If the stone is quite soft, the river can carve a deep, steep-sided valley, or gorge. The Grand Canyon in Arizona is a massive gorge cut by the Colorado River. It is about 277 miles (446 km) long, and in areas it is up to 18 miles (29 km) wide and 1.1 miles (1.8 km) deep.

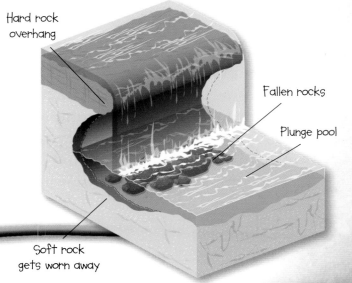

Hard rock overhang

Fallen rocks

Plunge pool

Soft rock gets worn away

◀ A waterfall forms where a river flows from hard rock onto softer rock. The softer rock is worn away faster, while the overhanging ledge of hard rock gradually crumbles away. Over time, the waterfall retreats, or moves upstream.

Record-breaking lakes

22 **The Caspian Sea in central Asia is actually the world's biggest lake!** It covers 149,200 square miles (386,400 sq km). It isn't connected to true seas and oceans, but because it's so big, and is salty like the sea, some experts say it isn't a proper lake, either. The world's biggest freshwater (non-salty) lake is Lake Superior, bordered by the United States and Canada.

▼ A picture of the Caspian Sea taken from space. Swirling clouds of sediment (sand and mud) and plankton (tiny plants and animals) can be seen.

Plankton and sediment

23 **The Dead Sea in Israel is another lake that is referred to as a sea.** At 1,300 feet (400 m) below sea level, it is the lowest lake in the world. The Dead Sea is very salty because no rivers flow out of it. All the salts and minerals that are washed into it remain there as the water evaporates in the Sun's heat. In fact the Dead Sea is nine times saltier than the real sea. It gets its name because no fish or other animals can live in such salty water.

24 **The world's deepest lake is Lake Baikal in Russia.** At its deepest point, it's 5,315 feet (1,620 m) deep. Because of this, it contains far more water than any other lake in the world. Twenty percent of all the unfrozen freshwater on Earth is in Lake Baikal.

▲ The high levels of salt in the Dead Sea mean that people can float easily in the water.

25 **The largest body of freshwater is found in North America.** On the border between the United States and Canada are the Great Lakes. They contain one-fifth of the world's freshwater– a staggering 6 quadrillion gallons (22.8 quadrillion l)!

26 **Many lakes around the world are believed to be home to mysterious monsters.** According to legend, a monster that looks similar to a plesiosaur lives in Loch Ness in Scotland. Plesiosaurs were prehistoric water reptiles that lived at the same time as the dinosaurs. Scientists think they became extinct (died out) 65 million years ago. However some people believe they may still live in Loch Ness.

CANADA

Lake Superior

Lake Huron

Lake Michigan

Lake Ontario

Lake Erie

UNITED STATES

◄ The five Great Lakes are situated in the United States and Canada. The biggest is Lake Superior, followed by Huron, Michigan, Erie, and Ontario.

Going underground

27 Humans have climbed the world's highest mountains — but many underground caves are still unexplored. Caves are usually formed by water flowing through cracks underground. The water slowly dissolves certain types of rock, such as limestone. Over thousands of years, it can hollow out deep shafts, tunnels, and even huge underground chambers.

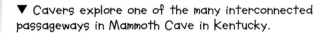
▼ Cavers explore one of the many interconnected passageways in Mammoth Cave in Kentucky.

28 A cave in Malaysia contains the world's biggest single underground chamber. The Sarawak Chamber measures 2,300 feet (700 m) long, 1,300 feet (400 m) wide and at least 230 feet (70 m) high. You could line up eight Boeing 747 aircraft, nose to tail, along its length — and still have space to spare.

29 The world's longest cave system is Mammoth Cave in Kentucky. It has at least 400 miles (643 km) of passageways — but explorers keep discovering more. Some experts think that only a small part of the whole cave has been explored.

▼ Caves form over thousands of years as water flows through cracks in underground rocks.

1. Rainwater seeps into cracks in rocks   2. Water dissolves rock, forming channels   3. Over time, large cave systems develop

◀ A view inside the Sarawak Chamber in Malaysia, the biggest cave chamber in the world.

30 In 2005, cave explorers broke a record, traveling more than 1.2 miles (2 km) below Earth's surface. They were exploring the Voronya Cave in Georgia, near Russia. It is the deepest cave in the world, with a maximum depth of 7,020 feet (2,140 m).

31 Workers in a mine in Mexico discovered an amazing cave by accident in 2000. They were drilling a tunnel when they found a large chamber filled with enormous crystals. The crystals are made of the mineral gypsum. They look like giant swords, measuring 6.5 feet (2 m) wide by up to 36 feet (11 m) long. The chamber, which is around 980 feet (300 m) deep, is now known as the Cave of Crystals.

▶ A geologist (a scientist who studies the Earth and its rocks) stands inside the amazing Cave of Crystals in Mexico.

I DON'T BELIEVE IT!

The cave salamander of central Europe is a type of amphibian. It spends its entire life in dark caves and its eyes have become blind as a result.

Extreme earthquakes

32 **An earthquake happens when the Earth's crust moves suddenly.** The crust trembles, cracks, or lurches up and down. Earthquakes can be disastrous. They make houses fall down, tear roads apart, and destroy bridges. They can also cause tsunamis.

33 **Earthquakes happen because the Earth's crust is like a jigsaw.** It is made up of several huge pieces called tectonic plates. The plates fit together quite neatly, covering the Earth. However they can squeeze and push against each other. Sometimes, this pushing makes the plates slip and move suddenly, causing an earthquake.

Fault line

Focus

Shock waves

▶ Earthquakes often happen when two tectonic plates slip and grind against each other. The focus is the point where the plates suddenly move.

▼ Earthquake waves travel through and across the ground in four different ways.

1. Primary waves stretch then squeeze the ground

2. Secondary waves shake the ground from side to side

3. Raleigh waves move in ripples up and down across the surface

4. Love waves travel across the surface moving the ground from side to side

▲ The San Andreas fault in California is a crack in the Earth's crust where two tectonic plates join. It has been the scene of several major earthquakes.

► Damage caused by an earthquake in Kobe, Japan, 1995. It measured 7.2 on the Richter Scale and killed more than 6,000 people.

34 **Earthquakes can flatten whole cities and kill thousands.** One of the deadliest earthquakes ever hit the city of Tangshan, China, in 1976. Most of the city's buildings were destroyed, and at least 240,000 people died. In 2003, an earthquake destroyed the ancient city of Bam in Iran. Over 70 percent of its buildings fell down and around 30,000 people were killed.

35 **Scientists measure earthquakes using the Richter scale.** It records the amount of energy that an earthquake releases. The biggest quakes are not always the most dangerous – it depends where they happen. In a big city, a quake measuring 4 or 5 on the scale could do more damage than a quake measuring 8 or 9 in the countryside.

36 **There are things you can do to stay safer during an earthquake.** For example, if you are outside, you should keep away from buildings and power lines. If you are indoors, you should find shelter under a strong table. Some places also have quake-proof buildings.

I DON'T BELIEVE IT!

Since ancient times, people have noticed animals behaving strangely just before earthquakes. Dogs and cats can get agitated, and herds of cattle have been known to run away.

▼ As there are a lot of earthquakes in Japan, school children regularly practice what to do if an earthquake strikes.

Terrifying tsunamis

37 **A tsunami is a giant wave or series of waves.** Tsunamis form when a large amount of water in a sea or lake is moved suddenly. This sets up a circular wave, a bit like the ripples you see when you throw a pebble into a pond. The wave then zooms outwards until it hits land.

▼ A tsunami wave crashes onto the promenade on Ao Nang Beach, Thailand, in 2004. The power and speed of a tsunami can easily sweep away cars and even entire buildings.

▶ A tsunami begins as fast-traveling waves far out at sea. As they approach land, the waves slow down, but become much taller.

As the tall tsunami reaches shallow water, it surges forward onto the shore

38 **When a tsunami hits, it can smash the coast to smithereens.** Out in the ocean, tsunami waves are very long, low, and fast-moving. However as a tsunami moves into shallow water, the wave slows down. All the water in it piles up, forming a powerful wall of water, often between 30 and 100 feet (10 and 30 m) high. As it crashes onto the shore, it can flood towns, tear up trees, and sweep away cars, buildings, and people.

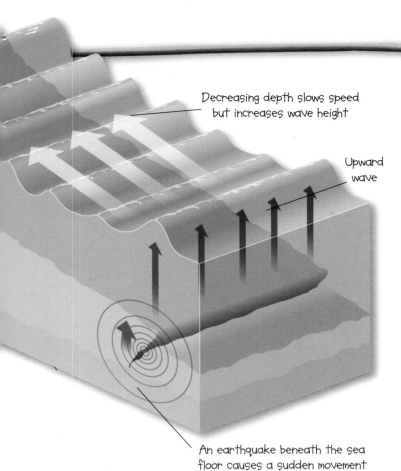

Decreasing depth slows speed but increases wave height

Upward wave

An earthquake beneath the sea floor causes a sudden movement of a massive column of water

40 **The tallest tsunami was higher than a skyscraper.** It occurred at Lituya Bay in Alaska in 1958. An earthquake triggered a landslide, and rock and soil plunged into the sea. A giant tsunami, over 1,640 feet (500 m) high, zoomed down the bay. Luckily, there were no towns there, but the wave stripped the coast of trees. A giant tsunami such as this is sometimes called a mega-tsunami.

39 **Most tsunamis are caused by earthquakes under the sea.** A section of seabed shifts suddenly, and the water above it is jolted upwards. Tsunamis can also happen when a landslide or volcanic eruption throws a large amount of rock into the sea, pushing the water aside. This happened when Krakatau, a volcano in Indonesia, erupted in 1883. The tsunamis it caused killed 36,000 people.

41 **A tsunami in the Indian Ocean in 2004 was the deadliest ever recorded.** It was caused by a huge undersea earthquake near the coast of Indonesia. Tsunami waves spread across the ocean and swamped coasts in Indonesia, Thailand, Sri Lanka, India, and the Maldive Islands. Around 230,000 people were killed.

▼ The town of Kalutara in Sri Lanka, shown in satellite images before (left) and after (right) being swamped by the deadly 2004 tsunami.

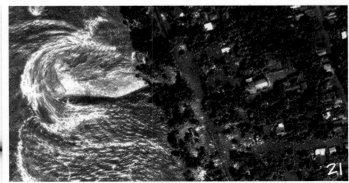

Dry deserts

42 Deserts occur in places where it's hard for rain to reach. Most rain comes from clouds that form over the sea and blow onto the land. If there's a big mountain range, the clouds never reach the other side. An area called a rain shadow desert forms. Deserts also form in the middle of continents. The land there is so far from the sea, rain clouds rarely reach it.

▲ The Namib Desert in the southwest of Africa contains some of the biggest sand dunes in the world.

43 The world's biggest desert used to be a swamp! The Sahara takes up most of northern Africa. It is made up of over 3,300,000 square miles (8,500,000 sq km) of dry sand, pebbles, and boulders. There are some oases too, where freshwater springs flow out of the ground. Animal bones and objects left by ancient peoples show that around 6,000 years ago, the Sahara was green and swampy. Lots of hippos, crocodiles, and humans lived there.

▼ These sand piles show the relative sizes of the world's biggest deserts.

Patagonian Desert
260,000 square miles
(670,000 sq km)

Kalahari Desert
360,000 square miles
(930,000 sq km)

Gobi Desert
500,000 square miles
(1,300,000 sq km)

Arabian Desert
900,000 square miles
(2,300,000 sq km)

Sahara
3,320,000 square miles
(8,600,000 sq km)

▲ Desert roses aren't plants. They occur when desert minerals, such as gypsum, combine with sand to form crystals.

▶ Sand dunes form in different shapes and patterns, depending on the type of wind and sand in the desert. The blue arrows indicate the wind direction.

44 Deserts aren't always hot. The hottest temperature ever recorded was 136°F (57.8°C) in Libya. However deserts can be cold, too. The average temperature in the Atacama Desert, South America, is only about 50°F (10°C). In the Gobi Desert in Asia, winter temperatures can drop to -40°F (−40°C). All deserts can be cold at night, as there are no clouds to stop heat escaping.

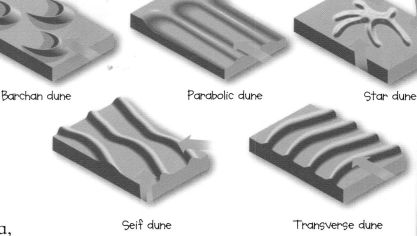

Barchan dune

Parabolic dune

Star dune

Seif dune

Transverse dune

45 The world's driest desert is the Atacama Desert in Chile, South America. This desert is right next to the sea! It formed because, in South America, rain clouds blow from east to west. They drop their rain on the Amazon rainforest, but cannot get past the Andes mountains. On the other side of the Andes, next to the Pacific Ocean, is the Atacama Desert. It is so dry that people who died there 9,000 years ago have been preserved as mummies.

▶ An oasis is a freshwater spring in a desert. Oases form when water stored deep underground meets a barrier of rock that it can't soak through and rises to the desert surface.

46 Even in dry deserts, there is water if you know where to look. Desert plants, such as cactuses, store water in their stems, leaves, or spines. When rain does fall, it seeps into the ground and stays there. Desert people and animals chew desert plants or dig into the ground to find enough water.

The ends of the Earth

47 **The Earth is round, but it has two "ends" – the North Pole and the South Pole.** The Earth is constantly spinning around an imaginary line called the axis. At the ends of this axis are the poles. Here, it is always cold, because the poles are so far from the Sun.

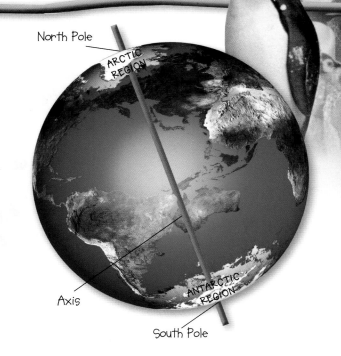

▲ The position of the poles means they receive little heat from the Sun.

48 **At the North Pole, the average winter temperature is −30°F (−34°C).** At the South Pole, it's much colder in winter – averaging −78°F (−61°C). It's hard for humans to survive in this cold. Water droplets in your breath would freeze on your face. If you were to touch something made of metal with your bare hand, it would freeze onto your skin and stick there.

49 **The area around the North Pole is called the Arctic.** Parts of Europe, Asia, and North America reach into the Arctic, but most of it is actually the Arctic Ocean. Many animals live in the Arctic. Polar bears and seals live on the ice and Arctic foxes, Arctic hares, and snowy owls live on the land. The sea around the pole is mainly frozen. Scientists have found the ice is melting because of global warming. This is happening because pollution in the air is trapping heat close to the Earth, making it warm up.

◀ Pollution in the form of carbon dioxide gas traps heat from the Sun, making the Earth warm up. This is one reason that the polar ice is melting.

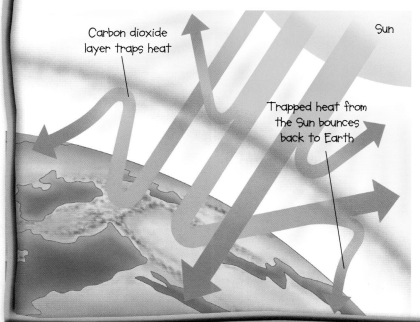

Carbon dioxide layer traps heat

Sun

Trapped heat from the Sun bounces back to Earth

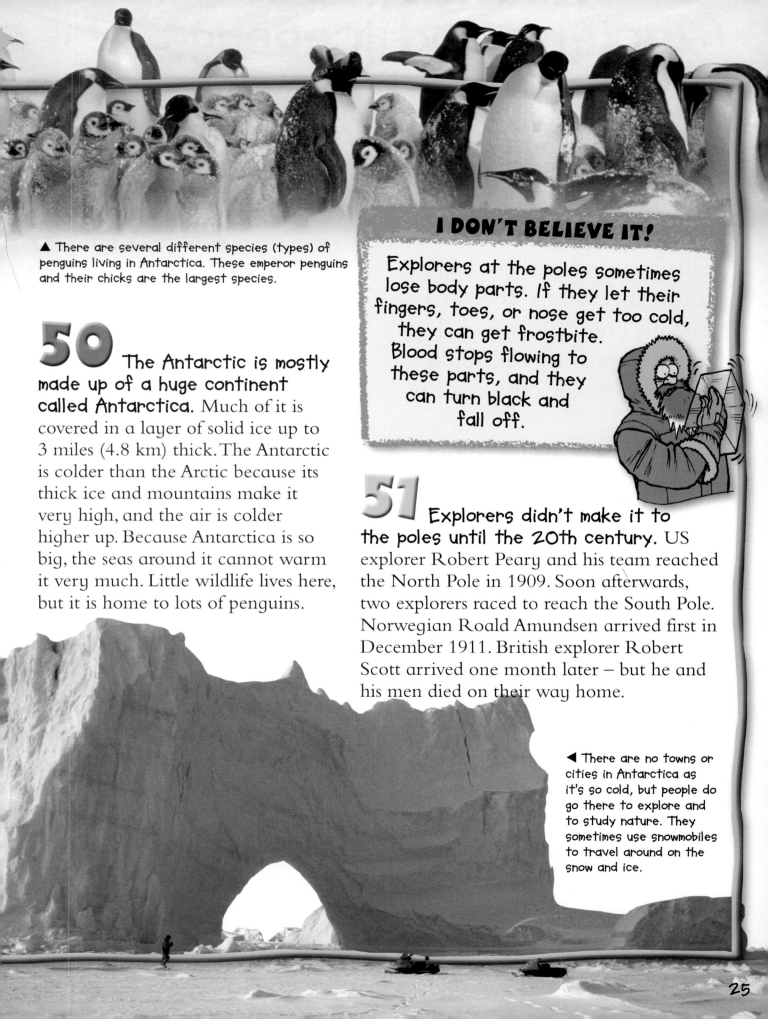

▲ There are several different species (types) of penguins living in Antarctica. These emperor penguins and their chicks are the largest species.

I DON'T BELIEVE IT!

Explorers at the poles sometimes lose body parts. If they let their fingers, toes, or nose get too cold, they can get frostbite. Blood stops flowing to these parts, and they can turn black and fall off.

50 **The Antarctic is mostly made up of a huge continent called Antarctica.** Much of it is covered in a layer of solid ice up to 3 miles (4.8 km) thick. The Antarctic is colder than the Arctic because its thick ice and mountains make it very high, and the air is colder higher up. Because Antarctica is so big, the seas around it cannot warm it very much. Little wildlife lives here, but it is home to lots of penguins.

51 **Explorers didn't make it to the poles until the 20th century.** US explorer Robert Peary and his team reached the North Pole in 1909. Soon afterwards, two explorers raced to reach the South Pole. Norwegian Roald Amundsen arrived first in December 1911. British explorer Robert Scott arrived one month later — but he and his men died on their way home.

◄ There are no towns or cities in Antarctica as it's so cold, but people do go there to explore and to study nature. They sometimes use snowmobiles to travel around on the snow and ice.

Glaciers and icebergs

52 About two percent of the water in the world is permanently frozen as ice. The ice is found at the chilly polar regions and on high mountains where the air is freezing cold. On steep slopes, the ice creeps downhill, like a very slow river. This kind of ice "river" is called a glacier. On high mountains, glaciers flow downhill until they reach warmer air and start to melt. At the poles, many glaciers flow into the sea.

▼ Instead of melting on the way down a mountain, this glacier in Prince William Sound, Alaska, is flowing into a fjord.

▶ A glacier develops deep cracks called crevasses as it moves downhill. The lower end of a glacier is called the "snout."

Snout

Crevasse

53 One of the world's biggest glaciers, not including the ice at the poles, is the Siachen Glacier in the Himalayas. It is 43 miles (70 km) long and, in places, its ice is over 330 feet (100 m) thick. India and Pakistan have been fighting a war over who the glacier belongs to since 1984. It has been home to hundreds of soldiers for more than 20 years.

54 Glaciers have shaped the Earth.
As a glacier flows down a mountain, the heavy ice pushes and scrapes at the soil and rocks. This carves a huge, U-shaped valley, known as a glacial valley. Twenty thousand years ago, when the Earth was in an Ice Age, glaciers covered much more of the land than they do now. Since then, many have melted, revealing their glacial valleys.

55 Icebergs exist because of glaciers.
At the poles, glaciers flow downhill to the sea. There, the ice is slowly pushed out into the water, where it starts to float. Every so often, a large chunk of the glacier breaks off and floats away into the sea. This is an iceberg, and it drifts until it melts.

56 Icebergs are a problem for ships.
As an iceberg floats, only about one-tenth of it sticks up out of the sea. The rest is below the surface. Many icebergs have odd, lumpy shapes. This means that a ship can bump into the underwater part of an iceberg, even if the part above water looks far away. Icebergs have damaged and sunk many ships, including the famous ocean liner *Titanic* in 1912.

▼ These penguins are on an iceberg in the Southern Ocean, close to Antarctica. A huge mass of ice can be seen below the water's surface.

MAKE AN ICEBERG

You will need:
plastic container   clear bowl   water

1. Fill the container with water and put it in the freezer.
2. When frozen, remove your 'iceberg' from the container.
3. Fill the clear bowl with water and place your iceberg in it.
4. Look through the side to see how much of your iceberg is underwater and what shape it makes.

Amazing oceans

57 About 70 percent of the Earth's surface is covered by ocean. The oceans cover about 139 million square miles (361 million sq km), and they are all connected. The average depth of the ocean is 12,080 feet (3,680 m). Over 90 percent of the Earth's species (types) of living things live in the oceans.

58 The deepest point in all the world's oceans is called Challenger Deep. It is in the Mariana Trench in the Pacific Ocean and is 6.8 miles (10.99 km) deep. A tower of 3,500 elephants, one on top of the next, could stand in it without touching the surface. In 1960, two explorers, Jacques Piccard and Don Walsh, visited the bottom of Challenger Deep in a diving vessel called *Trieste*.

59 If you were sitting at the bottom of the deep ocean, you'd be squashed flat. At great depths, the weight of all the water above presses from all sides. At the bottom of Challenger Deep, the water pressure is more than 1,000 times stronger than at the surface. It's cold, too – only just above the freezing point. People can only go there inside specially built diving machines with thick walls that can resist the pressure and cold.

▲ The *Trieste*, which made the deepest deep-sea dive ever in 1960, was made of a large tank full of gasoline to give buoyancy, with a small round passenger chamber fixed underneath.

Underwater volcano

Ocean ridge

Oceanic crust

Deep-sea trench

Challenger Deep

► This map shows the ridges, trenches, plains, and mountains within the world's oceans, as well as those on land.

ARCTIC OCEAN

ATLANTIC OCEAN

PACIFIC OCEAN

INDIAN OCEAN

SOUTHERN OCEAN

60 One of the world's most extreme environments is found under the sea.

At hydrothermal vents, incredibly hot water bubbles out from inside the Earth at temperatures of up to 750°F (400°C). Around the hot vents live unusual creatures, such as giant tubeworms and sea spiders, and tiny bacteria that feed on the minerals dissolved in the hot water. Hydrothermal vents were only discovered in 1977.

▼ A cross-section of the seabed. It usually slopes gently away from the shore, then drops steeply down to a flat plain.

61 Sea level – the height of the sea – is about the same all over the world.

It changes over time, as the Earth's temperature varies. About 20,000 years ago, during the Ice Age, the sea level was about 425 feet (130 m) lower than it is now. At the moment, the sea level is rising because global warming is making ice melt at the poles.

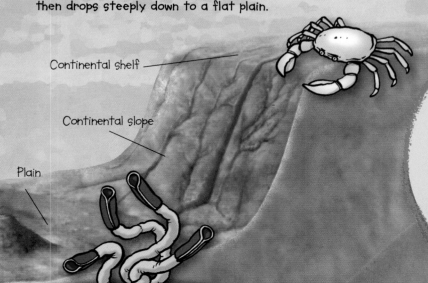

Continental shelf

Continental slope

Plain

TRUE OR FALSE?

1. Challenger Deep is deeper than Mount Everest is tall.
2. The water at the bottom of the sea is always very cold.
3. Sea creatures bigger than blue whales could exist.

Answers:
1. True, Everest is only 5.5 miles (8.9 km) high
2. False – the water can be hot around hydrothermal vents
3. True – the sea is so big, it could contain species unknown to science

Raining cats and dogs

62 **It may seem like bad weather, but we need rain.** Rain happens because the Sun's heat makes water in the sea evaporate. It turns into a gas, rises into the air, and forms clouds. The clouds then blow over the land. They cool down, turn back into water, and fall as rain. If this didn't happen, there would be no life on Earth – all living things need water to survive.

▲ Heavy rain is accompanied by big, black clouds.

64 **In rainforests it rains almost every day.** Rainforests are found in the warm tropical parts of the Earth, near the Equator. The hot sunshine makes lots of water evaporate and fall as rain. A lot of the rain that falls on a rainforest never touches the ground. It collects on the treetops, then evaporates into the air, before falling as rain again.

63 **The world's rainiest place is Meghalaya, an area of northeast India.** Some towns there, such as Cherrapunji and Mawsynram, get around 453 inches (11,500 mm) of rain a year. If the rain didn't drain away or evaporate, it would be 38 feet (11.5 m) deep after one year!

MAKE A RAIN GAUGE

You will need:
jar or food container with a flat base and straight sides   ruler   notebook

1. Find a good place to put your container in a shady spot away from buildings.

2. Dig a small hole in the ground to fit it into, or put stones around it to hold it in place.

3. Each day at the same time measure the depth of the water, then empty your container.

4. Record your results in a notebook to keep

▼ Water continually rises from the sea into the air, falls on the land as rain, then flows back to the sea. This is called the water cycle.

As clouds cool down, they turn back into liquid water and fall as rain

Water evaporates from plants and the ground

Rainwater flows into rivers and back into the sea

Water evaporates from the sea and blows over the land

65 It doesn't really rain cats and dogs — but there have been reports of red rain and showers of frogs, fish, and crabs. Frogs and toads were reported falling in Minneapolis in 1901. It has rained fish in Singapore, and crabs in the United Kingdom. These strange showers probably happen when tornadoes or strong winds sweep up water containing living creatures, which then fall to the ground.

▼ A rickshaw driver and passenger travel through monsoon floods in India. When rains are heavy, streets turn to rivers and people's homes may be washed away.

66 A monsoon is a very rainy season. Monsoons happen in parts of Asia, especially India, in late summer. The land gets very hot and heats the air above it. The hot air rises, and this sucks in damp, cloudy air from the sea. The clouds rush over the land. When they meet the Himalayan mountains, they rise and get colder. This creates lots of rain, especially in northern India.

67 **Lightning is a giant spark of electricity.** It happens when tiny droplets of water and ice swirl around inside a storm cloud. This makes the cloud develop a strong electrical charge. Eventually, a spark jumps between the base of the cloud and the ground. This allows electricity to flow, releasing the electrical charge. We see the spark as a flash or "bolt" of lightning.

Positive charge

Negative charge

Negative charge from the cloud meets a positive charge from the ground to create lightning

▲ During a thunderstorm, negative electrical charge builds up at the base of a cloud, while the ground has a positive charge. A lightning spark jumps between them to release the charge.

I DON'T BELIEVE IT!

At any one time, there are around 2,000 thunderstorms happening on Earth. Lightning strikes somewhere in the world about 100 times every second.

68 **Thunder and lightning go together.** In fact, thunder is the sound of lightning. When a lightning bolt jumps through the air, it is very hot. It can reach a temperature of 54,000° (30,000°C). It heats the air around it very quickly. Heat makes air expand (get bigger). It expands so suddenly that it pushes against the air around it and creates a shock wave. The wave travels through the air, and our ears detect it as a loud boom.

69 Long ago, people used to think lightning was a punishment sent by their gods. However, from the 1500s, scientists began learning about electricity and how it worked. Around 1750, US scientist Benjamin Franklin found that lightning was a kind of electricity. He invented the lightning rod to protect buildings from lightning damage. It is a metal pole that can be fixed to tall buildings. If lightning strikes, the electrical charge runs down the pole and down a metal wire, then flows safely into the ground.

◄ You can clearly see the lightning rod on the spire of this cathedral in Liverpool, England.

70 Lightning can strike the same person twice — or more. A US park ranger named Roy Sullivan was struck by lightning seven times during his life. It is quite rare for lightning to strike people and most of those who are struck survive. However lightning does kill over 2,000 people around the world each year.

▼ Fulgurites occur when lightning strikes sand. The high temperature makes the sand melt. It eventually cools into hollow tubes.

71 Lightning can make glass. Glass is made by heating up sand. When lightning strikes in a sandy desert or on a sandy beach, this happens naturally. At the place where the lightning hits the ground, it creates a tubelike tunnel of glass in the sand. These natural glass tubes are called fulgurites.

Hammered by hail

72 Hail doesn't happen often – but it can be one of the scariest kinds of weather. When it hails, balls of hard, heavy ice fall out of the sky. Hailstones are usually small, about the size of peas. However they can be bigger – marble-sized, egg-sized, or even tennis-ball–sized. Sometimes they're big enough to crush crops, smash car windows, or even kill people.

▼ A man shows off scars on his back – the result of being hit by hailstones while riding a bicycle.

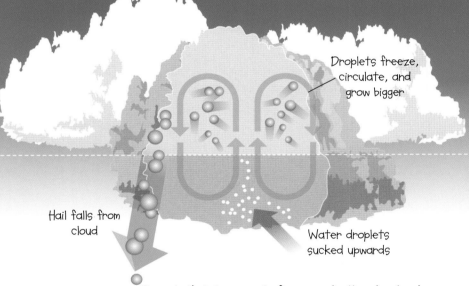

Droplets freeze, circulate, and grow bigger

Water droplets sucked upwards

Hail falls from cloud

▲ Hailstones only form inside thunderclouds. Eventually they become too heavy and fall to the ground as lumps of ice.

73 A hailstone needs a seed. Hailstones form inside thunderclouds when very cold water droplets freeze onto a tiny object – the "seed." It could be a speck of dust or a plant seed carried into the sky by the wind. The tiny hailstone is then tossed around by strong winds inside the cloud. More and more layers of ice build up around it, until it is so heavy that it falls to the ground.

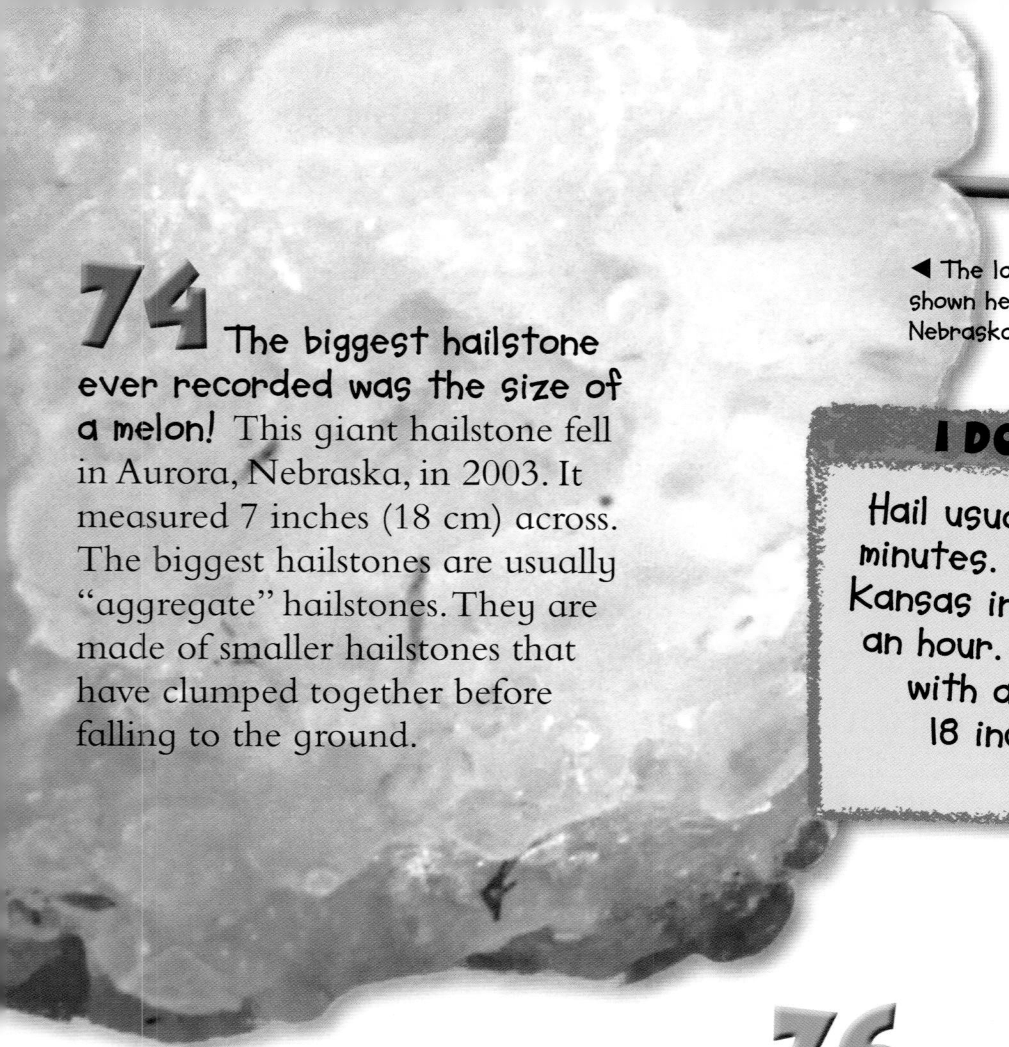

74 **The biggest hailstone ever recorded was the size of a melon!** This giant hailstone fell in Aurora, Nebraska, in 2003. It measured 7 inches (18 cm) across. The biggest hailstones are usually "aggregate" hailstones. They are made of smaller hailstones that have clumped together before falling to the ground.

◄ The largest hailstone on record is shown here at actual size. It fell in Nebraska in 2003.

I DON'T BELIEVE IT!

Hail usually only falls for a few minutes. However, a hailstorm in Kansas in 1959 went on for over an hour. It covered the ground with a layer of hailstones 18 inches (46 cm) deep!

75 **Sometimes a hailstone forms around a living thing.** A farmer in Quebec, Canada reported finding a frog inside a hailstone in 1864. In 1894, a hailstone with a turtle inside was reported to have fallen on Bovina, Mississippi. Smaller creatures such as spiders and flies are often trapped inside hailstones.

76 **The world's worst hailstorms happen in Northern India and Bangladesh.** Hailstones often destroy crops, and people are regularly injured and killed. In 1888, a hailstorm in India killed around 250 people and more than 1,000 sheep and goats.

► People in Mexico City, Mexico, shovel hailstones after a huge hailstorm on August 3, 2006.

Extreme snow and ice

77 **An ice storm isn't stormy – but it is dangerous.** Cold rain falls onto freezing cold surfaces. The rain freezes solid, forming a thick layer of ice on the ground, trees, and other objects. Ice storms cause "black ice"– invisible ice on roads that causes accidents. Ice-laden trees fall down, breaking power lines and cutting off roads.

◀ Overburdened by the weight of ice from an ice storm, this tree has collapsed across a road.

▲ An avalanche thunders downhill in Silverton, Colorado. This avalanche was started deliberately by dropping explosives, in order to make the mountains safer for visitors.

78 **An avalanche is a massive pile of snow crashing down a mountainside.** Avalanches can happen whenever lots of snow piles up at the top of a slope. They can be deadly if the snow lands on top of mountain walkers or skiers. Sometimes, big avalanches bury whole houses or even whole villages.

79 **A blizzard, or snowstorm, is even more dangerous than an ice storm.** If you get caught outdoors in a blizzard, it's very easy to get lost. Falling snow fills the air, making it impossible to see. Thick snowdrifts build up, making it hard to walk or drive. People have lost their way and died in blizzards, just a short distance from safety.

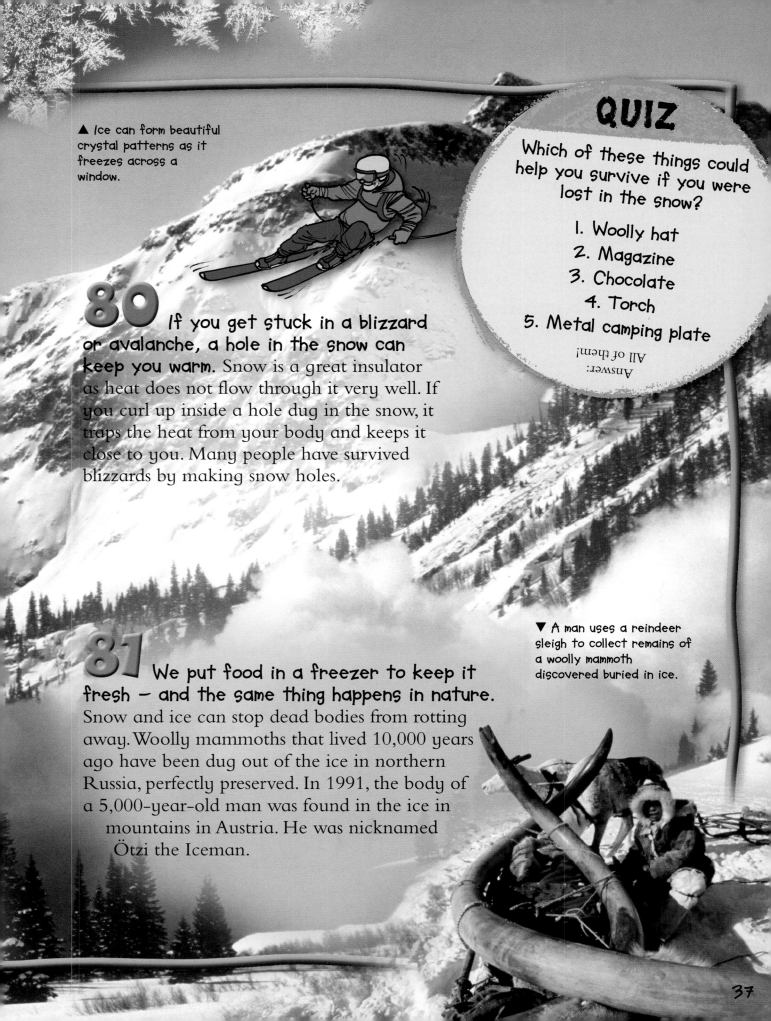

▲ Ice can form beautiful crystal patterns as it freezes across a window.

QUIZ

Which of these things could help you survive if you were lost in the snow?

1. Woolly hat
2. Magazine
3. Chocolate
4. Torch
5. Metal camping plate

Answer:
All of them!

80 **If you get stuck in a blizzard or avalanche, a hole in the snow can keep you warm.** Snow is a great insulator as heat does not flow through it very well. If you curl up inside a hole dug in the snow, it traps the heat from your body and keeps it close to you. Many people have survived blizzards by making snow holes.

▼ A man uses a reindeer sleigh to collect remains of a woolly mammoth discovered buried in ice.

81 **We put food in a freezer to keep it fresh — and the same thing happens in nature.** Snow and ice can stop dead bodies from rotting away. Woolly mammoths that lived 10,000 years ago have been dug out of the ice in northern Russia, perfectly preserved. In 1991, the body of a 5,000-year-old man was found in the ice in mountains in Austria. He was nicknamed Ötzi the Iceman.

Twisting tornadoes

82 **Tornadoes are also called twisters.** A tornado is an incredibly powerful windstorm that twists around in a swirling "vortex" shape. It forms a narrow funnel or tube, stretching from the clouds to the ground. Tornadoes often look dark because of all the dirt, dust, and broken objects that they pick up as they travel across the land.

83 **You can sometimes tell when a tornado is coming, because the sky turns green.** Tornadoes usually develop from thunderclouds. Scientists are not sure exactly how they form. They think that as warm, damp air rises, drier, colder air is pulled in and begins to swirl around it. This creates a spinning tube of wind that moves along the ground. A tornado can travel at up to 50 miles (80 km) an hour.

84 **Tornadoes contain some of the fastest winds on the planet.** Wind inside a tornado can move at up to 300 miles (500 km) an hour. This powerful wind can cause terrible damage. Tornadoes smash buildings, tear off roofs, make bridges collapse, and suck out doors and windows. They can pick up people, animals, and cars, and carry them through the air. In 2006, a tornado in Missouri picked up 19-year-old Matt Suter and carried him nearly 1,300 feet (400 m). He survived with only cuts and bruises.

Cold front

Warm front

◀ Tornadoes often form where a front, or mass, of cold air meets warm air. They spin around each other and form a funnel shape.

▲ A large, terrifying tornado snakes down to the ground from the base of a big thundercloud.

85 Damaging tornadoes happen most often in Tornado Alley. This is an area which stretches across the middle of the United States, between the states of Texas and Illinois. Tornadoes are most common there in the tornado season, from April to August. The Great Tri-State Tornado of 1925 was one of the worst ever. It roared through Missouri, Illinois, and Indiana, traveling 215 miles (350 km). It destroyed 15,000 homes and killed 695 people.

◀ The shaded area on this map shows the part of the USA known as Tornado Alley, where tornadoes are most common.

86 Sometimes, tornadoes occur in deserts or over the sea. In sandy deserts, small tornadoes pick up sand and carry it along in a whirling tower. They are called sand devils or dust devils. Tornadoes over the sea can suck up water in the same way and carry it for long distances. They are known as waterspouts.

Howling hurricanes

▶ A man struggles through the high winds of Hurricane Andrew that hit the United States in 1992. Only Hurricane Katrina in 2005 has been more destructive.

87 **A hurricane is a huge, swirling mass of storm clouds.** Hurricanes form over the ocean, but often travel onto land where they cause floods and destroy whole towns. A typical hurricane is about 300 miles (500 km) wide. In the middle is a small, circular area with no clouds in it, about 30 miles (48 km) wide. This is called the "eye" of the hurricane.

88 **Hurricanes begin in the tropics where the ocean is warm.** The ocean surface has to be about 80°F (27°C) or warmer for a hurricane to start. Warm, wet air rises, forming rainclouds. These begin to swirl in a spiral, caused by the spinning Earth. If the winds reach 74 miles (119 km) an hour, the storm is called a hurricane. Hurricane winds can be as fast as 150 miles (240 km) an hour.

89 **Hurricanes have names!** Each year, all hurricanes are given names from a list. There are six lists altogether, so the same names are repeated every six years. If a hurricane becomes famous – like Hurricane Katrina in 2005 – the list is changed so that name does not reappear.

I DON'T BELIEVE IT!

At the "eye" of a hurricane, in the middle of the storm, it's calm and quiet, not stormy at all. The eye only lasts a short time, until the rest of the storm arrives.

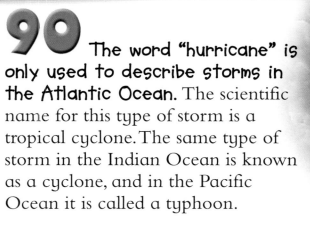

90 The word "hurricane" is only used to describe storms in the Atlantic Ocean. The scientific name for this type of storm is a tropical cyclone. The same type of storm in the Indian Ocean is known as a cyclone, and in the Pacific Ocean it is called a typhoon.

91 Hurricanes and other tropical cyclones can cause terrible disasters. When Hurricane Katrina struck the southern coast of the United States in August 2005, it damaged many cities on the coasts of Mississippi and Louisiana. In New Orleans, huge waves broke through the flood barriers and more than 80 percent of the city was flooded. The hurricane killed over 1,800 people and caused damage costing over $80 billion. The Bhola cyclone, which hit Bangladesh in 1970, killed over 300,000 people.

▲ A satellite view from space showing a hurricane swirling across the Gulf of Mexico.

92 Scientists think hurricanes are getting worse. Global warming means that the Earth's temperature is rising, so the seas are getting warmer. This means that more hurricanes are likely. Hurricanes are also becoming bigger and more powerful, as there is more heat energy to fuel them.

▼ These buildings near Lake Pontchartrain, Louisiana, were destroyed by Hurricane Katrina in 2005.

Water, water everywhere

93 A flood happens when water overflows and covers what is normally land. Floods can be caused by rivers overflowing their banks after heavy rain. The sea can also flood the land with large waves or tsunamis. Floods can be useful – some rivers flood every year in the rainy season, bringing water and mud that make farmland moist and fertile. However most floods are bad news.

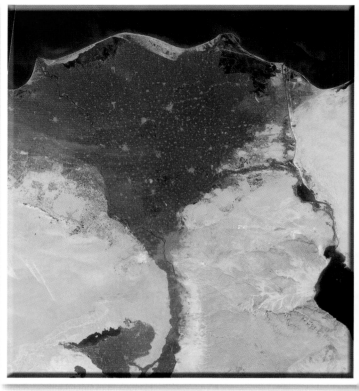

▲ A satellite image of the Nile River in Egypt flowing into the Mediterranean Sea. The green triangular area is the Nile Delta. The Nile used to flood each summer, spreading fertile silt across the land. These floods are now controlled by the Aswan Dam in southern Egypt.

▼ A woman carries a precious pot of clean drinking water through dirty floodwaters during a flood in Bangladesh in 1998.

94 Floods can cause death and destruction. When floodwater flows into houses, it fills them with mud, garbage, and sewage (smelly waste from drains and toilets). It ruins electrical appliances, carpets, and furniture. After a flood, homes have to be completely cleaned out and repaired – costing huge amounts of money. Even worse, fast-flowing floodwater can sweep away people, cars, and even buildings.

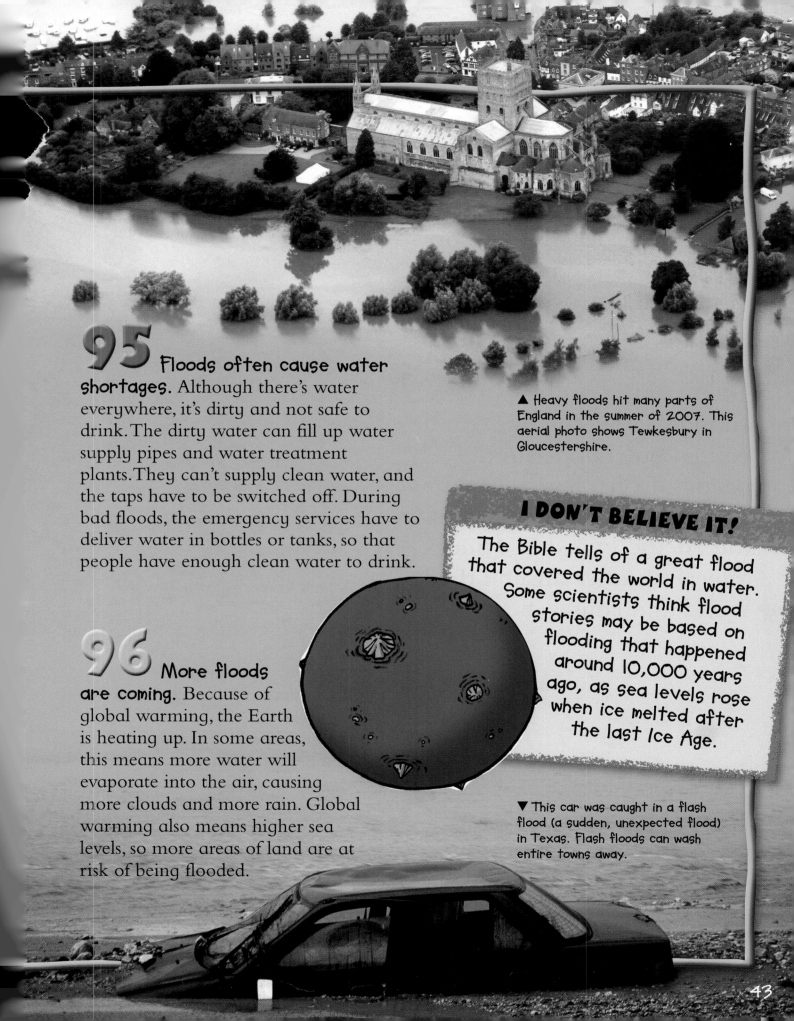

95 **Floods often cause water shortages.** Although there's water everywhere, it's dirty and not safe to drink. The dirty water can fill up water supply pipes and water treatment plants. They can't supply clean water, and the taps have to be switched off. During bad floods, the emergency services have to deliver water in bottles or tanks, so that people have enough clean water to drink.

▲ Heavy floods hit many parts of England in the summer of 2007. This aerial photo shows Tewkesbury in Gloucestershire.

96 **More floods are coming.** Because of global warming, the Earth is heating up. In some areas, this means more water will evaporate into the air, causing more clouds and more rain. Global warming also means higher sea levels, so more areas of land are at risk of being flooded.

I DON'T BELIEVE IT!

The Bible tells of a great flood that covered the world in water. Some scientists think flood stories may be based on flooding that happened around 10,000 years ago, as sea levels rose when ice melted after the last Ice Age.

▼ This car was caught in a flash flood (a sudden, unexpected flood) in Texas. Flash floods can wash entire towns away.

43

Disastrous droughts

97 A drought is a shortage of rainfall that leaves the land dry. Deserts hardly ever get rain and are dry and dusty all the time. A drought happens when a place gets much less rain than usual. Scientists don't always know why weather patterns change. However, this can be caused by changes in the oceans. Every few years, a change in sea temperatures in the Pacific, called El Niño, affects weather around the world and causes droughts.

▲ During drought conditions, water is precious. Without it, people, animals, and plants will die.

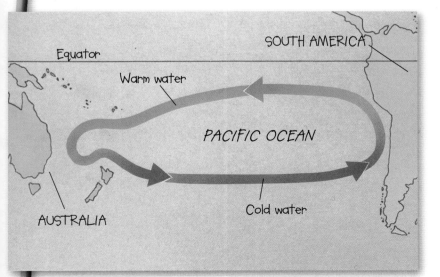

▲ El Niño is a warming of surface ocean waters in the eastern Pacific that can lead to flooding and drought around the world.

98 Droughts are disastrous for people, animals, and plants. A shortage of rain means crops can't grow properly, and herds of animals can't get enough drinking water. So people face food and water shortages. Dried-out grass and trees can easily catch fire, and loose dust can blow up into blinding dust storms. Droughts can also cause wars when people are forced to leave their lands and flock into other areas.

▲ Part of the Murray River in southern Australia, usually flowing with water, lies empty during a drought.

99 **Droughts have always happened.** They are mentioned in many ancient books, such as the Bible and the writings of the ancient Mesopotamians, who lived in the area around what is now Iraq. However, scientists think that today global warming is making some droughts worse. As the world gets warmer, weather patterns are changing. Some areas, such as eastern Australia, are now having worse droughts than they used to.

100 **The "Dust Bowl" was a great drought disaster that hit the United States in the 1930s.** Several years of drought dried out farm soil in the central states, such as Oklahoma and Kansas. It blew away in huge dust storms, and farmers could not grow their crops. Hundreds of thousands of people had to leave the area. Many trekked west in search of new lives and jobs.

TRUE OR FALSE?

1. Droughts make forest fires more likely.
2. The Dust Bowl is a volcano in the United States.
3. El Niño is a temperature change in the Indian Ocean.

Answers:
1. True. Droughts make forests drier so they burn more easily 2. False. The Dust Bowl was a drought 3. False. El Niño is in the Pacific Ocean

◀ A massive dust storm about to engulf a farm during the Dust Bowl years. Caused by drought conditions, these storms devastated the American prairies.

Glossary

agitate: to move or stir up

buoyancy: the ability of an object to float in water or air

dissolve: to mix something solid with a liquid so that it becomes part of the liquid

drench: to make something completely wet

dune: a hill of sand near an ocean or in a desert that is formed by the wind

engulf: to flow over and cover

fjord: a narrow part of the ocean between cliffs or steep hills or mountains

gorge: a narrow steep-walled canyon or part of a canyon

insulator: a material that allows little or no heat, electricity, or sound to go into or out of something

preserve: to keep (something) in its original state or in good condition

satellite: a machine that is sent into space and that moves around the earth, moon, sun, or a planet

silt: sand, soil, or mud that is carried by flowing water and sinks to the bottom of a river, pond, or other body of water

surge: to move very quickly and suddenly in a particular direction. Also, to suddenly increase to a high level.

torrential: coming in a very fast, very large stream

trek: to walk or travel for a long, often difficult distance

For More Information

Books

Kenah, Katharine. *Extreme! Earth*. Greensboro, NC: Cason-Dellosa Publishing, 2013.

Maisner, Heather. *Amazing Weather*. Columbus, OH: School Specialty, 2007.

Reynolds, Toby, and Paul Calver. *Extreme Earth*. London, England: Franklin Watts, 2013.

Websites

BBC Earth—Extreme Earth
www.bbc.co.uk/science/earth/collections/extreme_earth
See video clips and read more about extreme Earth places and events.

Extreme Earth Photo Gallery
photography.nationalgeographic.com/photography/photos/extreme-earth/
Check out National Geographic's extreme Earth photos.

Extreme Earth Quiz
travel.nationalgeographic.com/travel/countries/superlative-earth-quiz/
Test your knowledge—take an extreme Earth quiz!

Index